21st Century Skills *INNOVATION* *Library*

Sports Broadcasting

by Michael Teitelbaum

INNOVATION IN

Published in the United States of America by Cherry Lake Publishing
Ann Arbor, Michigan
www.cherrylakepublishing.com

Content Adviser: William Hoon, PhD, Associate Professor, Department of Broadcasting, Western Illinois University

Photo Credits: Cover and page 3, ©Roger Bamber/Alamy; page 4, ©Paul Yates, used under license from Shutterstock, Inc.; page 7, ©Black Star/Alamy; pages 8 and 17, ©ClassicStock/ Alamy; page 10, ©North Wind Picture Archives/Alamy; page 13, ©moodboard/Alamy; page 14, ©Corbis Super RF/Alamy; page 18, ©iStockphoto.com/ImagineGolf; page 20, ©John Simmons/ Alamy; page 22, ©Eileen Langsley Olympic Images/Alamy; page 23, ©David Hodges/Alamy; pages 25, 27, and 28, ©AP Photo

Library of Congress Cataloging-in-Publication Data
Teitelbaum, Michael.
 Sports broadcasting / by Michael Teitelbaum.
    p. cm.—(Innovation in entertainment)
Includes index.
ISBN-13: 978-1-60279-216-6
ISBN-10: 1-60279-216-X
1. Television broadcasting of sports—Juvenile literature. 2. Radio
broadcasting of sports—Juvenile literature. 3. Television broadcasting of
sports—Technological innovations—Juvenile literature. 4. Radio
broadcasting of sports—Technological innovations—Juvenile literature. I.
Title. II. Series.
GV742.3.T45 2009
070.4'49796—dc22   2008008951

Cherry Lake Publishing would like to acknowledge the work of
The Partnership for 21st Century Skills.
Please visit www.21stcenturyskills.org for more information.

CONTENTS

CHAPTER ONE

From Megaphones to Cable

The batter stepped up to the plate. The pitcher delivered his pitch. The batter swung and hit a deep drive over the fence for a home run. A crowd of fans hundreds of miles from the ballpark listened to the play-by-play and cheered.

But this game was not broadcast on television or even on radio. The year was 1873. It was 47 years before the first radio station went on the air. The details of this game weren't sent over the airwaves,

The pioneers of sports broadcasting couldn't have imagined the leaps in technology that would occur in just a few decades.

but through telegraph wires. The person receiving the telegraph signal from someone at the ballpark used a **megaphone** to announce what was happening to the crowd.

When radio came along, the broadcasting of sports became one of the first things to go out over the new wireless airwaves. The first sporting event broadcast on the radio was a boxing match heard by listeners of WWJ in Detroit, Michigan, on September 6, 1920.

In August 1921, KDKA in Pittsburgh, Pennsylvania, started broadcasting Pittsburgh Pirates baseball games. Two months later, the first World Series (which was between two New York teams) was broadcast on WJZ in New York City.

Most sports broadcasts were re-creations. Information from an event was sent by telegraph

Learning & Innovation Skills

In 1921, radio and television innovator David Sarnoff was working for RCA. He learned that General Electric (GE) was planning to deliver a powerful portable radio transmitter to the U.S. Navy. Hoping to sell more of RCA's radios by providing more interesting programs, Sarnoff convinced GE to loan him the transmitter. The transmitter was carried by train to a railroad terminal in Hoboken, New Jersey. A telephone line was then run to a boxing arena 2.5 miles (4 kilometers) away. That was where a heavyweight championship fight was taking place between champion Jack Dempsey and challenger Georges Carpentier. An announcer at the fight reported the action over the phone line to a technician at the transmitter. The technician then broadcast what was happening from a tiny metal shack at the train station.

What do you think happened next? Do you think Sarnoff's plan was a good idea?

or telephone lines to a radio station. A radio announcer would **dramatize** the information, adding sound effects such as crowd noise or the crack of a bat.

The first coast-to-coast broadcast took place in 1927. It was the Rose Bowl college football game. For the first time in history, people across the United States heard about an event at the same time it was happening.

By the early 1930s, radio had become an important part of everyday American life. Major national sporting events—such as heavyweight boxing championships, the Rose Bowl game, and the Kentucky Derby horse race—linked people from coast to coast through radio. By the end of the decade, the next major innovation in sports broadcasting was television. Now sports fans could see their favorite teams and athletes.

One of the first things to be shown on television was a sports event. On May 17, 1939, just a few weeks after NBC started broadcasting the first television signals, it televised a college baseball game. The game was between Princeton and Columbia universities. By August, a Major League Baseball game was broadcast. For the first time, those not at the ballpark could watch the stars of the nation's most popular sport.

The 1940s saw additional steps forward. In 1946, the first four-city hookup allowed more than 100,000 fans along the East Coast to watch Joe Louis battle Billy

Early sports commentators used a type of binoculars to see players better. Today, television monitors help give announcers a better view of the action.

Conn for the heavyweight boxing championship. The following year, an astounding 3.9 million people watched the World Series when it was televised for the first time. At that time, a television was considered a luxury item. Most people couldn't afford one. Instead, they watched the games at bars or by standing in front of the windows of **appliance** stores that sold televisions.

During the 1950s, the popularity of television skyrocketed as TVs became more affordable. The year 1951 saw the beginning of live, coast-to-coast TV broadcasting. People on one side of the country could watch sporting events from the other coast. By 1954,

Television made it possible for viewers to see a sporting event without having to be at the event.

90 percent of the United States was receiving television broadcasts and more than half of U.S. homes had TVs. By the end of the 1950s, television had replaced radio as the standard for receiving sports broadcasts in the home.

The 1960s brought innovations in the types of sports events that were covered. The Summer Olympics were broadcast on TV for the first time in 1960. This brought the achievements of athletes from around the world into people's living rooms.

In the 1970s, cable TV brought signals to those who previously couldn't receive broadcasts. Satellites in space beamed sporting events all around the globe. In September 1979, the ESPN sports network began broadcasting. Now fans could watch games and news from the sports world 24 hours a day.

Today, high-definition televisions allow viewers to watch the sports they love in crisp, clear detail. The technology has changed through the years. But the **impulse** among sports fans to know what happened at the big game has been there since the days of the telegraph.

CHAPTER TWO

Innovations in Technology and Equipment

Morse's telegraph was an important step in the development of rapid, long-distance communication.

The invention of the telegraph by Samuel F. B. Morse in 1844 marked the beginning of the age of long-distance communication. Alexander Graham Bell's telephone, invented in 1876, added the human voice to the mix. When radio swept the nation in the 1920s, mass communication—one voice speaking to many listeners—began. And sports were there each step of the way.

In the days of the telegraph, reports of baseball games were common. A telegraph operator, known as a telegrapher, would attend the game. The operator sent reports of each play using Morse Code, a series of dots and dashes that was used to send messages. Another telegrapher at the other end of the wire would read the report of the game to an eager crowd.

Radio's great innovation was that it allowed fans to enjoy an announcer's description of the action in the comfort of their own homes. But the way the announcer got his information hadn't changed much.

Telephone lines were also used to report sports events. Someone at the sports event would describe the action over the telephone to an announcer at a radio station. The announcer would then repeat what had just been heard into the microphone for listeners at home.

Life & Career Skills

One of the dangers of re-creating games on the radio using telegraph lines was the risk of losing the telegraph connection. Ronald Reagan, who was president of the United States from 1981 to 1989, once worked as a sportscaster. He did re-creations of Chicago Cubs baseball games. During one game in 1935, his radio station lost its telegraph connection in the bottom of the ninth inning, with the score tied. For six and a half minutes, with no information coming to him from the ballpark, Reagan told his listeners that the batter was fouling off pitch after pitch. When the telegraph signal finally returned, Reagan picked up the action as if no problem had occurred. His ability to improvise, remain calm under pressure, and adapt to an unexpected problem served him well in his political career.

Eventually, radio stations began sending announcers to the ballpark, stadium, arena, or track. Their voices were still carried by a telephone line, only now those lines were connected to the radio station's transmitter. This allowed fans to hear the play-by-play action as it happened, from the person who was actually watching the event.

Television came along in the late 1930s and changed everything. But the first sports broadcasts looked nothing like the games on TV today. The picture quality was fuzzy, and only one camera was used. Also, fewer TVs existed, so not as many people saw the broadcast.

The United States' entry into World War II in December 1941 delayed technical innovation in television. The talents of researchers, engineers, and scientists were needed for the war effort. When the war ended in 1945, these technical innovators got busy improving cameras, transmitters, and TVs.

By 1948, coaxial cable, a thick rope of wires capable of carrying television pictures and sound, linked Boston, New York, Philadelphia, and Washington, D.C. This allowed a clear signal of an event to be broadcast live in all four cities at the same time.

How did people in the rest of the country see the event? They had to wait several days for a **kinescope** of the event to arrive. A kinescope is a film made of a TV

Advances in camera technology allowed different sports to be broadcast. Underwater cameras made it possible to film water sports from new angles.

screen that is broadcasting an event. The result was fuzzy, but at the time it was the only way to create a record of a TV show. By 1951, the broadcasting industry took a major step toward solving this problem. That year, coaxial cable finally linked the East and West coasts. Now viewers on either coast could watch a live game from anywhere in the country.

In 1956, the Ampex Corporation introduced a
technical innovation that changed television sports—the
videotape recorder. It produced a record of an event
instantly, with a much clearer image than kinescopes had.
Videotapes could also be copied easily, so tapes of games
could be sent all over the country. This innovation made
instant replays possible. For the first time, a great play

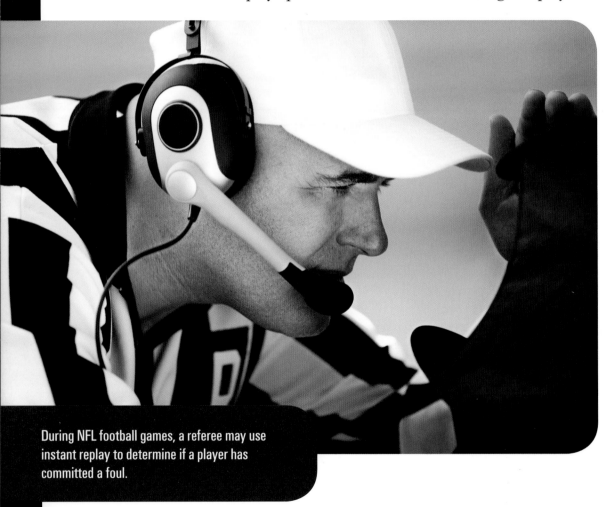

During NFL football games, a referee may use
instant replay to determine if a player has
committed a foul.

could be shown again, immediately after it happened. As this technology improved, slow-motion replay came along, as well as the ability to view a play from many different angles.

By 1960, smaller, lighter broadcasting equipment allowed TV crews to travel farther to bring sporting events from more remote locations to more people. Microwave dishes mounted on trucks could beam signals directly from stadiums back to radio and TV stations for broadcast.

In 1962, the Telstar satellite was launched into space, connecting the entire world. For the first time, people in Europe could watch an American baseball game. And people in the United States could watch the Le Mans Grand Prix d'Endurance car race, live from France.

The **merger** of computer technology with television brought many innovations in the way sports are shown on TV. Now, during a football game, computers can add colored lines on the TV screen showing where the line of **scrimmage** and first-down markers are. A computerized **graphic** can show exactly where a baseball pitch lands and if it's inside or outside the strike zone. Computers can also add bright color to a hockey puck to make it easier to follow on TV.

CHAPTER THREE

Announcing the Games

The basic use of sports broadcasting has been the same regardless of technology. It doesn't matter whether the signal was sent by telegraph, radio, or television. A sports broadcast has always been about telling sports fans what happened in a particular sporting event. Sometimes this means live coverage so that the fans can follow the action as the event is occurring. Other times, the information comes in the form of news reports and **analysis** once the game is over.

In the early days of sports on the radio, the great innovators were the play-by-play announcers. They painted pictures with words, filling listeners' minds with the images and emotions of what was going on at the event.

The first great sports play-by-play announcer was Graham McNamee. In the early 1920s, he covered everything from boxing matches to baseball games. McNamee excited listeners with his colorful reports. More than simply stating what had happened, he talked about the crowd and the atmosphere at the event. His descriptions helped listeners imagine that they were there, too.

When television began broadcasting sports, its technical limitations helped determine which sports were covered. Only one camera was used in the early days. This made sports played on big fields, such as baseball and football, difficult to broadcast. So boxing and wrestling **dominated** the sports airwaves in the 1940s and early 1950s.

In 1961, an innovator in sports programming named Roone Arledge brought a program called *Wide World of Sports* to ABC television. It featured a variety of sports

Many boxing matches were televised in the 1940s and 1950s.

from all over the world. Viewers got to see faraway places and athletes they might never have seen without the show. Most of the sports shown were filmed or taped in advance. This allowed dramatic moments to be presented in a storylike manner. Even those who didn't usually watch sports enjoyed the show and helped make it a hit.

But it wasn't just the format that made *Wide World of Sports* so popular. Jim McKay was hired to be the show's host. In 1968, his talent was recognized when he won the first Emmy ever presented to a sports broadcaster. In 1972, McKay's skills were put to the test as he broadcast coverage of the terrorist attack at the Munich Olympic games. His calm under pressure earned him two Emmy awards that year—one for sports broadcasting and one for news coverage of the terrorist attack.

Camera crews try to get the best possible shots without disturbing athletes.

In 1970, Arledge brought *Monday Night Football* to ABC. The program captured new fans and increased the popularity of the game. People tuned in as much for the fun conversation among the show's three colorful hosts as they did to watch the game.

Around that same time, cable TV came along. At first, this new method of delivering a TV signal was used to get TV to remote locations that didn't get good reception. But in 1979, an innovator named William F. Rasmussen came up with the idea of a 24-hour cable channel devoted entirely to sports. ESPN was born. Now sports fans could see games, get reports, and stay up-to-date on the latest in the sports world anytime they wanted. This changed both sports broadcasting and cable television forever.

Learning & Innovation Skills

Jackie Robinson broke baseball's color barrier by joining the Brooklyn Dodgers in 1947. Legendary Dodger broadcaster Red Barber was raised in the southern United States, where **discrimination** was more common than in the North. Barber was unsure about whether black baseball players should play alongside white players. He communicated his concerns to Dodgers owner Branch Rickey. Rickey explained to Barber that Barber's personal opinions didn't matter. Barber had been hired only to tell listeners what was happening on the field. Barber understood that he needed to think of Robinson simply as a baseball player, not as a *black* baseball player. Barber set aside his personal opinions and focused on Robinson's athletic abilities on the field. As a result, Barber went on to become one of the most accurate and impartial announcers in sports history. He also became one of Robinson's biggest supporters.

CHAPTER FOUR

Business Innovations

The World Cup receives heavy coverage from photographers and camera crews. The soccer tournament is broadcast to millions of viewers around the world.

In 1873, in Cleveland, Ohio, a telegraph company asked the owners of the local baseball team for permission to enter the stadium to report play-by-play of the game. The team said no, that it owned the rights to the entertainment value of its games. **Undeterred**, the company's telegraph operator climbed a tree that overlooked the ball field. He plugged into a telegraph line and tapped away in Morse Code to transmit the game.

The issue of who owns the rights to a team's games carried over to radio. At first, the games were considered news events and were available for coverage. But in 1929, American League baseball team owners discussed banning all radio coverage of their games. Radio stations were making money by selling advertising time during their broadcasts of games. So the owners reasoned that the teams should get paid for providing the "product" the stations were broadcasting.

By the early 1930s, many radio stations were paying for the rights to broadcast sports events. This was formalized in 1936. The court ruled that sports teams could legally sell rights to their games. It said that only stations that paid for those rights could broadcast the games.

With the growth of television, the business of sports took off. Sports leagues and broadcasters realized that they could make a lot of money from the broadcast of

21st Century Content

From the beginning of television sports, TV networks have paid sports leagues for the rights to broadcast their games. The networks sell airtime to advertisers who want to run their commercials during the sports events. Today, pay-per-view has emerged as a new way to finance the broadcast of sporting events. Using cable TV technology, viewers order a particular event and pay a one-time fee to watch it. Pay-per-view events have proven very popular for boxing matches and for college basketball and football games not shown on free TV.

games. Prices paid for the rights to broadcast those games skyrocketed.

Today, broadcasters pay millions of dollars to professional sports leagues, college sports associations, and Olympic committees for the rights to broadcast events on radio and television. Major sports leagues such as the NFL make most of their money from broadcast

Creative camera use helps crews get interesting shots. This camera is mounted on a rock to film an Olympic canoe event.

Some of the programs with the most viewers in the history of television have been Super Bowl games.

rights fees, not from sales of tickets to the games themselves. Radio and TV stations and networks then sell airtime to advertisers for even more money. Running a 30-second commercial during the Super Bowl costs an advertiser more than $2 million.

CHAPTER FIVE

Famous Innovators

Many people have contributed to making sports broadcasting as popular as it is today. Here are just a few.

Graham McNamee

In 1923, a young radio announcer named Graham McNamee stepped up to the microphone in the Polo Grounds baseball stadium in New York City. He was there to cover the World Series between the New York Giants and the New York Yankees. During these broadcasts, he created the art of sports play-by-play announcing. Before McNamee, radio coverage of live sports events was handled by newspapers reporters. Their bland, "just the facts" approach proved boring to listeners. McNamee's skill for describing both the action on the field and the atmosphere within the ballpark in colorful,

Graham McNamee's skill was his ability to provide lively descriptions of sporting events and make listeners feel as if they were there.

creative terms attracted listeners. He changed what it meant to be a sports play-by-play announcer.

Walter "Red" Barber

Equally comfortable doing play-by-play on radio or TV, Red Barber broadcast the first televised baseball game in 1939. Barber was known for telling it like he saw it. He never rooted for the home team on the air, always presenting a fair view of the action. He was known for his colorful catchphrases such as "Oh, Doctor!" (for a great play) and "What a rhubarb!" (for a fight on the field). His eye for detail and smooth, impartial style helped him become one of the most influential announcers in sports history.

Roone Arledge

Roone Arledge believed that television coverage needed to do more than just show the action on the field. He knew he had to make viewers feel as if they were actually at a sporting event rather than just watching reporting on TV.

He applied this idea to ABC's coverage of college football and then created *Wide World of Sports* in 1961. His innovation of using taped events from around the world allowed him to turn sports competitions into dramatic stories that engaged even those who weren't big

Red Barber broadcast professional baseball for more than 30 seasons.

sports fans. In 1970, he brought *Monday Night Football* to the air and changed America's sports-viewing habits. By blending sports and entertainment, Arledge expanded the audience for ABC's sports broadcasts.

Part of what made announcer Howard Cosell memorable was his detailed analysis and quirky personality.

William F. Rasmussen

In 1979, William F. Rasmussen, a former sportscaster for the New England Whalers hockey team, came up with an idea. Along with his son Scott, he started the first all-sports network—ESPN. Using satellite technology, ESPN broadcast many games from different sports. It also introduced a show called *Sports Center*. This nightly report, modeled after a network newscast, focused only on sports. Within a few years, Rasmussen's idea had changed the way fans watched sports on television and opened the door for other cable TV networks.

Life & Career Skills

Howard Cosell was a successful New York lawyer in the 1950s. He was also a big sports fan, and many of his clients were professional athletes. After volunteering to host a radio program about Little League baseball, he decided to adapt his talents and begin a new career. He became a full-time sports broadcaster. Over the next 40 years, he became one of the most respected sportscasters in America. His commentaries were heard on ABC radio for many years. He covered the career of boxer Muhammad Ali and reached his peak as part of the original broadcast team of *Monday Night Football*.

Glossary

analysis (uh-NAL-uh-siss) a detailed explanation or discussion of something

appliance (uh-PLYE-uhnss) a machine that helps make a task easier or that entertains

discrimination (diss-krim-uh-NAY-shun) unfair opinions of others based on race, gender, religion, or other factors

dominated (DOM-uh-nate-id) controlled

dramatize (DRAM-uh-tize) to explain something in an exciting manner

graphic (GRAF-ik) a visual image

impulse (IM-puhlss) the desire to do something

kinescope (KI-neh-skope) a film made of a TV screen to create a record of a TV program

megaphone (MEG-uh-fone) a funnel-shaped device for increasing the volume of a voice

merger (MUR-jur) to bring together two or more things

scrimmage (SKRIM-ij) the point on a football field where the ball is placed at the beginning of a play

undeterred (uhn-di-TURD) not bothered by

For More Information

BOOKS

Ferguson Careers in Focus. *Broadcasting*. New York: Ferguson Publishing Company, 2007.

Meisenheimer, Mark. *No Pants Required: A Behind-the-Scenes Look at Television Sports Broadcasting*. Tucson, AZ: Wheatmark, 2007.

WEB SITES

American Sportscasters Online
www.americansportscastersonline.com/BroadcastFirsts.html
Learn more about sports broadcasting history

The Museum of Broadcast Communications
www.museum.tv/
Find out more about television and radio broadcasting

Index

About the Author

Michael Teitelbaum has been a writer and editor of children's books and magazines for more than 25 years. In addition to his fiction work, with characters ranging from Garfield to Spider-Man, Michael's most recent nonfiction books include *Mountain Biking*, *Rock Climbing*, and *Skiing* for Cherry Lake. Michael's latest work of fiction is *The Scary States of America*, published by Delacorte in 2007. Michael and his wife, Sheleigah, live in New York City.